TRADERS AND EXPLORERS IN WOODEN SHIPS

Muslims and the Age of Exploration

A Supplementary Social Studies Unit for Grade Five

Written by Susan Douglass
Illustrated by Abd Al-Muttalib Fahemy and Susan Douglass

Goodwordkidz

Helping you build a family of faith

First published 1995 by
The International Institute of Islamic Thought (IIIT)
500 Grove St., 2nd Floor
Herndon, VA 20170-4735, USA
Tel: (1-703) 471 1133 / Fax: (1-703) 471 3922
E-mail: iiit@iiit.org / URL: http://www.iiit.org

First published by Goodword Books in 2003
Reprinted 2004
in arrangement with The International Institute of Islamic Thought
© The International Institute of Islamic Thought 1995

Goodword Books Pvt. Ltd.
1, Nizamuddin West Market
New Delhi 110 013
e-mail: info@goodwordbooks.com
Printed in India

www.goodwordbooks.com

Islamic School Book Project

IIIT is a cultural and intellectual foundation registered in the United States of America in 1981 with the objectives of providing a comprehensive Islamic outlook through elucidating the principle of Islam and relating them to relevant issues of contemporary thought: regaining the intellectual, cultural, and civilizational identity of the ummah through Islamization of the various disciplines of knowledge, to rectify the methodology of contemporary Islamic thought in order to enable it to resume its contribution to the progress of human civilization and give it meaning and direction in line with the values and objectives of Islam.

IIIT seeks to achieve its objectives by holding specialized academic seminars and conferences, supporting educational and cultural institutions and projects, supporting and guiding graduate and post-graduate studies.

The IIIT Islamic School Book Project supports the writing, publication, and distribution of books and other teaching material for schools as part of its effort to present the true picture of Islam in a factual objective way. These educational resources, developed under the general guidelines of the IIIT Islamization of Knowledge program, cover the following fields: Islamic Studies, Social Studies, Literature, Science and Mathematics. International collaboration and coordination with teachers, schools and organizations is assured through the International Forum for Education Resources for Islamic English-medium schools.

For more information contact:

The Director
IIIT Islamic School Book Project
International Institute of Islamic Thought (IIIT)
500 Grove St., 2nd Floor,
Herndon, VA 20170-4735, USA
Tel: (1-703) 471 1133 / Fax: (1-703) 471 3922
E-mail: iiit@iiit.org / URL: http://www.iiit.org

Susan Douglass is an American-born Muslim who accepted Islam in 1974. She received the Bachelor of Arts in History from the University of Rochester in 1972. She received the Master of Arts in Arab Studies from Georgetown University in 1992. She holds teaching certification in social studies from New York and Virginia.

She has taught in a variety of settings and subjects, beginning with volunteer work in Headstart in 1965. She taught and coordinated art classes in a summer youth program from 1970-72 in Rochester, NY. Since returning to the U.S. in 1984, from extended stays in Germany and Egypt, she resumed work in education. She has taught arts, crafts and story sessions in Muslim summer school programs for several years in Herndon, VA. As teacher and Head of the Social Studies Department at the Islamic Saudi Academy, Fairfax, VA, she taught both elementary and secondary social studies, built a supplementary resource library, and led in preparing a K-12 social studies curriculum utilizing both American and Arab resources for the Academy's accreditation. The current IIIT project was conceived and developed in the classroom. The author is involved in numerous other educational projects, including work as reviewer and consultant to major textbook publishers in the field of social studies. She has reviewed and offered revisions to the California History/Social Science Framework (1994) and the National History Standards Project (1994), in addition to various projects for the Council on Islamic Education in Fountain Valley, CA, including a book, *Strategies and Structures for Presenting World History, with Islam and Muslim History as a Case Study* (Council on Islamic Education, 1994.)

ADVISORY PANEL MEMBERS

Rahima Abdullah
Elementary Coordinator
Islamic Saudi Academy, Alexandria, VA

Dr. Kadija A. Ali
Educational Projects Coordinator
International Institute of Islamic Thought,
Herndon, VA

Jinan N. Alkhateeb
Social Studies Teacher
Islamic Saudi Academy, Alexandria, VA

Mrs. Hamida Amanat
Director of Education
American Islamic Academy
Curriculum Consultant
Al-Ghazaly School, Pine brook, NJ

Shaker El Sayed
Coordinator
Islamic Teaching Center, Islamic Schools
Department
Islamic Society of North America, Plainfield,
IN

Dr. Tasneema Ghazi
IQRA International Educational Foundation,
Chicago, IL

Dr. Zakiyyah Muhammad
Universal Institute of Islamic Education,
Sacramento, CA

ACKNOWLEDGEMENTS

Many people's efforts have contributed to producing this series of supplementary units for Social Studies. First, I am grateful to the International Institute of Islamic Thought (IIIT) for placing their confidence in me to undertake a project of this size and for providing all the financial and logistical resources needed for its completion. I would like to thank Dr. Mahmud Rashdan, under whose guidance this project began in 1988. His wisdom helped to set it on a solid foundation. Without constant support and encouragement by Dr. Omar Hasan Kasule, project director 1991-present, and Dr. Kadija Ali Sharief, project coordinator (1993-present), this unit would never have met the light of day.

This project has been much enhanced by the members of the Advisory Panel. In addition to offering guidance on the project as a whole, they have spent time and detailed effort on each individual manuscript. These brothers and sisters are all active education professionals with a broad range of experience and a long list of accomplishments.

May Allah reward by family and grant them patience for sacrificing some degree of comfort so that I, as wife and mother, might realize this goal. I owe special thanks to my husband, Usama Amer, for his constant help with the computer, with Arabic sources and many other matters of consultation. With regard to the writing and editing process, I thank my students at the Islamic Saudi Academy who fired my enthusiasm for writing, and who used this unit in the raw material stage. I thank the teachers and students at ISA and elsewhere who have used the manuscript for this unit in their classes and helped me to refine the material. Among the panel member/teachers who have done so are Rahima Abdullah and Jinan Al-Khateeb. I owe special appreciation to Andrea Thigpen, an art teacher who worked enthusiastically with me to develop numerous activities for the upper elementary grades. She prepared the illustrations for the project and assisted greatly in making the ship project a success in two very large, back-to-back classes. Gratitude is extended for editing help to Freda Shamma, Yusef DeLorenzo and Rabiah Abdullah, without whose help many mistakes and oversights would have been missed.

It has been a pleasure to work on several units with the illustrator, Abd Al-Muttalib Fahemy, who contributed his skill and dedication, bringing enthusiasm and a rare willingness to go the extra mile to research a sketch or detail for accuracy. Finally, thanks to the many people at Kendall/Hunt Publishing Co. who graciously met my many requests and turned tentative, complex and unfamiliar material into a finished product.

May Allah reward the efforts of sincere workers and of the teachers and students for whom this unit was written.

Susan Douglass
Falls Church, Virginia
September 1994

TABLE OF CONTENTS

Part I:

Teacher's Notes

INTRODUCTION

This unit is the sixth in a series of supplementary units for the Social Studies. It reflects the belief that "history" should be remebered because it makes sense and it is enjoyable, and that even young students should be introduced to skills and concepts of historical scholarship. The series is an effort to offer an accurate and critical treatment of Islam in those areas of the standard curriculum which deal with it directly, and to introduce it into areas where an understanding of the role of Muslims is an essential part of events.

An important requirement in the design of this supplementary series is that each unit feature skills and concepts typical for the scope and sequence of the social studies curriculum in its grade level. Topics are similarly chosen for their close relationship to typical courses offered at or near their grade level. The units are intended to fulfill the classroom teacher's need for curriculum materials reflecting a high level of historical scholarship and student interest without long hours of teacher research and preparation.

PURPOSE AND PLACEMENT OF THE UNIT

This unit is offered to upper elementary students as an introductory chapter to their first comprehensive study of American history. It may also be used as an adjunct to study of the European Age of Exploration in world history courses for upper elementary/middle school grades. It can be used as a supplement to or substitute for the textbook chapter which discusses America's origins in the Old World. It provides background for the period in which Europe reached out across the globe for the first time. This treatment attempts to go beyond the heroism and adventure stories about the Age of Exploration.

Most textbook treatments of the period utterly fail to place Europe in the context of its cultural and technological development relative to other civilizations. This unit shows how the Islamic lands formed a hinge between East and West. It investigates the major motivations and development of the technological means for exploration. It goes beyond the stereotyped image of conflict between Christians and Muslims to explain the fruitful cultural exchange which occurred over the centuries. It demonstrates how the cosmopolitan character of the Islamic civilization united the Old World in interdepedence, contributing to Europe's later technological, scientific, cultural and economic achievements. Finally, the unit shows how all technological and historic advances in human civilization are cumulative efforts to which many peoples have made important contributions.

Using legends about Christopher Columbus as a starting point, students are introduced to the background of European exploration. In five sections, students are given the context in which Europe's desire to explore emerged. In simple terms, they are shown the economic and cultural background of the period. Factors of religious and political conflict are discussed. The technological state of navigation in Europe is explained, and the text shows how developments in this field made exploration possible. Finally, the various elements which led to Columbus' idea of sailing west to reach the East are pulled together into an understandable explanation.

Two related concepts are introduced in the unit: how ideas spread among people of different lands and how trade works. The idea of cultural transmission is explained in simple examples—how scientific knowledge spreads, how urban culture and luxury spread, and how new inventions are built upon old ideas. Trade is discussed in some detail, giving an explanation of its basic mechanics. The concept of traders as transmitters of culture is explained and examples are given. Incidentally, the task of the historian is introduced, showing how legends, artifacts and primary source materials are combined to write "history."

Most students are fascinated by stories of early ocean voyages, treasure and adventure on the high seas. Features of the unit pick up on this interest. The filmstrip on ships and navigation gives colorful detail for reinforcement and enrichment of the student text. Worksheets are provided for content reinforcement and skill development. A simple, inexpensive project to build three-dimensional ships has been much enjoyed by students, and creates a festive atmosphere in the classroom when displayed. Teaching suggestions, document study and a reference section are provided for comprehension and enrichment.

SKILLS: The students will be able to:

1. Locate major lands and cities mentioned in the text on a map (See "Places to Remember").
2. Identify the continents of the "Old World" and tell why they carry that name.
3. List several means by which ideas, knowledge, and customs spread from one land to another.
4. Describe what merchants do and list several side-effects of their work.
5. Follow routes on a map and identify goods and means of transportation from a legend.

CONTENT: The students will be able to:

1. Compare legends about Columbus with factual background.
2. Describe how scientific knowledge and luxury goods entered Europe before Columbus' time.
3. Describe trade in the Old World before Columbus, tell what goods were traded by whom.
4. Describe religious conflict between Christians and Muslims and tell where it was carried out.
5. Tell why trade grew in Europe in the Middle Ages.
6. Compare trade and invasions, and understand that both can spread ideas.
7. Describe and list reasons for the European plan to go to Asia by a water route.
8. Tell how Henry the Navigator carried out his plan to explore the route to Asia.
9. Describe the art of sailing as known by Europeans, Vikings, and Arabs.
10. List some dangers of sailing on the open seas.
11. Trace the development of Europe's exploring ships, showing how ideas were borrowed.
12. Tell why Columbus sailed West, and list his two mistakes.

SECTION 1:
Legends about Columbus are only partly true.
It was known that the world is round by Greeks, Muslims.
This knowledge came to educated Europeans through Spain and Italy.
The Muslim lands were rich in learning and city life.
Italian cities traded around the Mediterranean.
Traders spread ideas as well as goods.

SECTION 2:
Marco Polo's book made people interested in China.
Europeans already knew about Chinese and other Eastern goods.
Italian traders bought them in the Muslim cities.
Europeans saw them in Spain.
Europe, Asia and Africa were called the "Old World."
Fear of invaders kept Europeans from travelling or trading.
Muslim traders brought the goods together from many trade routes.
Venice was the first Italian trading city.
European kings and the Pope sent an army to invade Muslim lands and spread the
    Christian religion.
The armies lost and came home.
Christians fought in Muslim Spain and won.
Both saw the better way of life and wanted it for themselves.
Trade between Europe and the Muslim merchants grew.
Merchants earn profit by carrying goods and selling at a higher price to cover their costs.
Eastern goods were very expensive but sold well.
Europeans wanted to bring the goods and make more profit.

SECTION 3:
The shortest route to the East was through the Muslim lands.
The Muslims would have increased trade with other Europeans.
Europeans wanted to stop trading with Muslims and bring goods from the East themselves.
Europeans wanted to spread Christianity.
Muslims completely controlled the trade and Islam was spreading.
It would be difficult to make the Europeans' plan succeed.
Prince Henry of Portugal wanted to look for an all-water route to the East, to go around
    Muslim lands and take over the trade.

SECTION 4:

Finding an all-water route was very difficult.

European sailers were afraid to sail into open seas.

Prince Henry started a school of navigation.

The Muslims had much knowledge about navigation.

They kept charts and maps and had advanced navigation instruments like the astrolabe and compass.

Henry brought Muslim and other scientists to his school.

Sailing was very difficult in those days.

Europeans sailed near the coast in small, heavy ships.

They needed a new kind of ship for exploration.

Inventors use ideas from the past to make new things.

Viking ships in the North were well designed.

They used oars and one square sail and were "clinker-built."

Later European ships copied Viking ships.

Arab Muslims sailed several kinds of ships.

They used two or three triangular sails and were sewn or nailed together.

Their hulls were smooth and light, "caravel built."

Henry's builders copied the hull and sails from the Viking ships.

The caravels were good ships for exploring.

Columbus used a caravel to go to the New World.

SECTION 5:

Henry died before the all-water route was found.

Vasco Da Gama sailed to India in 1498.

The Pope gave the Portuguese all the lands and people they found.

No other European kings could disobey the Pope and claim the lands.

Columbus gave the Spanish a chance to claim the lands by sailing East.

He thought the westward route was shorter.

He thought the world was smaller than it is.

He didn't know about the Americas.

Columbus sailed to the New World in 1492.

His discoveries made Spain the richest country in Europe.

TRADERS AND EXPLORERS IN WOODEN SHIPS

Muslims and the Age of Exploration

Written by Susan Douglass
Illustrated by Abd Al-Muttalib Fahemy and Susan Douglass

اللَّهُ الَّذِى سَخَّرَ لَكُمُ الْبَحْرَ لِتَجْرِىَ الْفُلْكُ فِيهِ
بِأَمْرِهِ وَلِتَبْتَغُوا مِن فَضْلِهِ وَلَعَلَّكُمْ تَشْكُرُونَ

Allah it is Who made the sea of service to you,
That the ships may run on it by His command,
And that you may seek of His bounty
And that perhaps you may be thankful. (Qur'an, 65:12)

WHAT IS THIS BOOK ABOUT?

Everyone who studies America's history learns about Christopher Columbus. People in the United States celebrate Columbus Day in October, remembering him as the first European to discover America. Most people know about Columbus from **legends**, or stories that are part truth and part fiction. In this book, we will look behind the legends. We will find out what the world was like in Columbus' time. We will see what people knew, where they traveled and traded, and what they dreamed about. You will read about sailing ships and traders bringing riches from faraway lands, about the plans of kings and princes, and about scientists working to help us understand the world. You will learn that people from many different lands helped each other learn about and explore the world.

Part II:

Student Text

What Did People Know About the World in Columbus' Time?

The most famous legend about Columbus says he proved that the world was round. Meanwhile, everyone laughed at him, believing that it was flat. In fact, in those days many educated people knew that the earth is round. Some ancient peoples even thought the world might be round. People like the Phoenicians and Carthaginians may have sailed around Africa and across the seas. Ancient people also studied the stars and planets to prove the earth was round. One of those ancient peoples was the Greeks, who gathered much scientific knowledge. Later people learned from them. They wrote books and carried this knowledge all around the lands of the Mediterranean Sea.

MUSLIM SCHOLARS BROUGHT KNOWLEDGE TO EUROPE

Hundreds of years after the Greeks, Muslims came into the lands around the Mediterranean Sea. Muslims practice the faith called Islam. Muslims ruled lands from Spain almost to China. You can see these lands on the map on page 14. Muslims picked up knowledge from many lands. They translated it into Arabic language. Scientists in Muslim lands studied this information. They used it to make new discoveries. Muslim scientists made progress in medicine, mathematics, astronomy and geography. This knowledge spread to many other lands.

How did this knowledge come to Europe, which was Columbus' home? Columbus was from Italy. The king and queen of Spain paid for his famous voyage. Both Spain and Italy had many contacts with Muslim lands.

This scene shows a seaport on the Mediterranean. Muslim merchants traded with Christian, Jewish and other merchants. They loaded the ships with precious goods like spices, coffee, cloth and jewels. On the Mediterranean, the Indian Ocean and in other waters, Muslim traders sailed to many ports. Their work helped build cities and spread Islam.

For 700 years, Muslims controlled most of Spain and Portugal. This land was called Al-Andalus. Between 716 and 1492 Muslims built beautiful gardens and palaces, like the Alhambra, in Granada. They built great cities like Cordoba, with famous universities. Muslim scholars (people who study to gain knowledge) lived in these places. They studied, read and wrote books. They kept large libraries. Scholars from other parts of the Muslim lands traveled to Al-Andalus, bringing more ideas and information. This was easy, since they all used the Arabic language. After many years, people in Christian lands of Europe translated these books into European languages. Europeans came to Spain to study. That is how inventions and science known in Muslim countries came to Europe.

TRADERS CARRIED GOODS AND IDEAS TO FARAWAY LANDS

The country called Italy sticks out into the Mediterranean Sea like a boot. It is an ideal place for people who trade by sea. Many Italians became traders. Two famous Italian trading cities were Venice and Genoa. Genoa was Columbus' home city. During his time, Italian ships brought goods across the Mediterranean between Muslim and Italian ports.

When people trade with each other, they exchange knowledge as well as goods. Traders carry ideas from one country to another. They visit different lands and eat strange foods. They see things people at home never get to see. They also learn languages, customs and laws used by their trading partners. During their travels, traders also see new inventions and hear about scientific discoveries.

Traders carry this knowledge to other ports and back to their home cities. Knowledge spreads across the land with the traders' goods. Scientists travel on trading ships to meet and learn from each other. Ideas, knowledge, people and goods were exchanged between the Muslim lands and Europe. In the next section, you will see how this trade made Europeans want to explore the world.

Scholars in Muslim lands gathered knowledge from many civilizations. They read and translated ancient and newer books into Arabic. Men and women wrote about those subjects and developed new knowledge, science and literature. Libraries with thousands of books were places where scholars met to share ideas.

Understanding Section 1:

1. How did people long ago learn that the world is round?
2. What did Muslim scientists do with knowledge gained in their new lands?
3. How do traders help to spread ideas?
4. Why was Italy an important trading country?
5. How did the Muslims' scientific knowledge come to Europe?

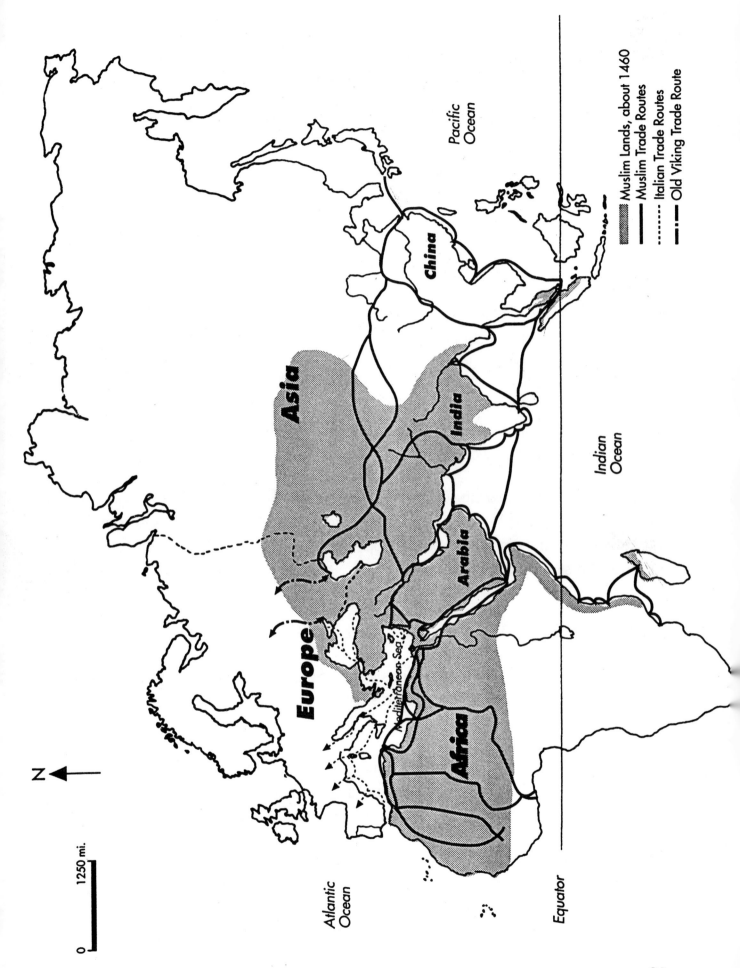

N

1250 mi.

0

Atlantic
Ocean

Africa

Europe

Mediterranean Sea

Arabia

Asia

India

China

Pacific
Ocean

Indian
Ocean

Equator

Muslim Lands, about 1460
Muslim Trade Routes
Italian Trade Routes
Old Viking Trade Route

Why Did Columbus Want to Travel to the Other Side of the World?

Another legend about Columbus is that Marco Polo's book made him dream of going to China. Marco Polo made a famous journey with his father to China. They lived there for many years. They saw many wonderful things not found in Europe. When he came home, Marco Polo wrote a book about his journey.

Like most legends, it is only partly true. Many people who read the book became interested in the lands he described. They wanted China's silk, fine dishes and a kind of powder that exploded when fire touched it.

Europeans already knew about goods from China. These things had been coming into Europe for a long time. Italian traders bought these goods from Muslims and sold them in Europe. Europeans also liked goods from the East and from Muslim Spain.

EUROPEANS DID NOT TRADE AND TRAVEL MUCH

How did Italians and Spanish Muslims get trade goods from the East? To answer, we need a map showing **trade routes** from the time before Columbus found America.

Europe, Asia and Africa, continents in the eastern half of the world, are called the "Old World." The rest of the world was unknown to Europeans until about 500 years ago. Europe is far to the west on the edge of the Old World.

Before Columbus, during a time called the Middle Ages, few Europeans traveled. For a long time, Europeans were afraid to travel because of **invaders** (people who move into other lands with armies). Europeans also fought among each other. They lived in strong castles where they made or grew

15

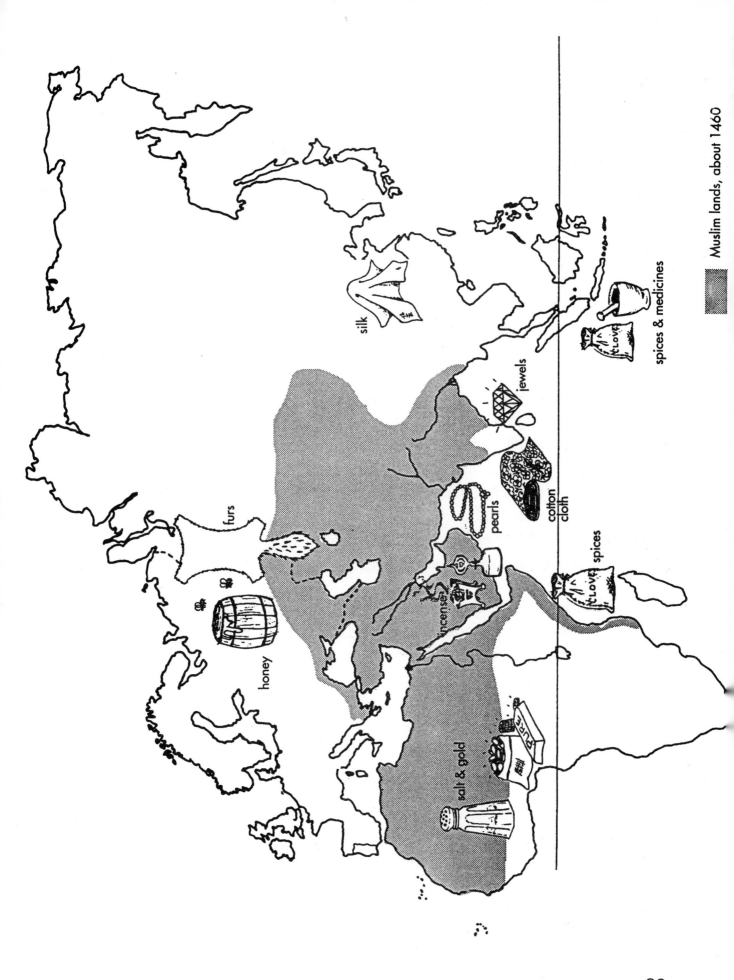

Muslim lands, about 1460

silk

spices & medicines

jewels

cotton cloth

pearls

spices

incense

furs

honey

salt & gold

23

everything they needed. They didn't even trade much with each other. At the same time in other lands, people were busy trading and traveling across the rivers, seas and deserts of the Old World.

TRADE ROUTES MET IN THE GREAT CITIES OF MUSLIM LANDS

The center of trade in the Old World was the Muslim lands. Rich, beautiful cities were filled with schools and hospitals, universities and great markets. These covered markets, called **bazaars**, were like modern shopping malls. Inside, shops were full of the aroma of spices, fruits and honey. Glass, fine dishes, silk and velvet cloth shone in bright colors. Gold and silver, pearls and precious jewels showed their glitter.

Merchants (another name for traders) brought these goods together from many places. Salt and gold were carried by camel caravans across the African desert. Viking traders carried honey, amber and furs down the long rivers of Russia to the Black Sea. Silk went by river boat, camel and donkey on the long journey from China. From lands around the Indian Ocean, ships from Muslim lands brought silk and cotton cloth, spices and medicines, woods, pearls and precious jewels. Huge camel caravans carried goods from Arabian ports to the Mediterranean Sea.

Great Muslim cities like Baghdad and Damascus, Cairo and Alexandria were centers of trade. There, **trade routes** (roads traders use to carry goods) came together from land and sea. In these cities, goods were sold for use all over the Muslim lands. Fabrics, glass, metals and jewels were made into fine goods for sale. Italian merchants also sailed to these great cities. They bought goods and carried them back to Europe. At first, only a few Italian cities like Venice sent ships. Then something made more Europeans want to buy goods from the East. You will read about what happened in the next pages.

THE CHURCH AND KINGS SENT ARMIES TO THE EAST

As time passed, some kings in Europe became very strong. The fighting in Europe began to die down. Roads grew safer. Farms grew more food. People

Many Muslim citites had bazaars, or covered markets like this one. Craftspeople worked here to make goods for sale. Merchants sold goods brought by caravans and ships from all over the Old World. People came to buy things, to browse, to hear the latest news and share ideas. Officials watched over fair prices, fair weights and measures, and quality. The openings in the domed ceilings pulled fresh air through the many gates and colonnades of the bazaar. It was natural air conditioning.

25

had more things to sell. They made wool and linen cloth, for example. Europeans began to trade more. Towns grew larger.

The Church in Europe also grew stronger. The Church wanted to spread the Christian faith. The leader of the Christian Church — the Pope — told European kings to prepare armies. He told them it was their duty to God to fight the Muslims. In Spain, Christian kings fought against the Muslims and took over some of their cities. The Pope wanted these armies to take over Jerusalem, which lay in Muslim territory. Jerusalem is a holy city for Christians, Muslims and Jews.

Kings and soldiers from all over Europe joined the Pope's armies. They tried to capture Jerusalem, in the land where Jesus was born. By land and sea, the Crusaders came. They won some battles, and they lost some. After several tries, the Popes and kings gave up. The armies went home. The Crusades lasted a long time. They did not reach their goal, but they brought many changes to Europe.

Soldiers returning home brought back stories and samples of the East's riches. They saw a better way of life in Muslim lands than they knew at home. They tasted food spiced with pepper, cloves and cinnamon. They brought back silk and cotton cloth that only kings could afford at home. Some had been treated in clean hospitals with medicines not found in Europe. Europeans began to want these things, too. Trade with Muslim merchants grew. More Italian cities began to send ships across the Mediterranean Sea for goods. Other countries began to join them.

SOME MERCHANTS GOT RICH, OTHERS GOT JEALOUS

The money that a merchant earns is called **profit**. He buys goods where they are made. He takes the goods to people who want them. On the way, he has to pay for transport. He pays taxes for soldiers who protect roads and harbors. He might lose his goods because of storms or robbers. When he sells the goods, he charges a higher price than he paid. The difference between what he paid and what he gets is called **profit**. This is how merchants make their living.

Even long ago, Muslim doctors practiced medicine in hospitals. They used medicines from plants grown in the hospital herb garden or brought from distant lands. They performed surgery with instruments they invented. Some of these are still used today. Poor people were treated without paying. Muslim doctors even treated some Christian knights during the Crusades. Muslim medical books were used in many lands.

27

Italian merchants had to pay Muslim merchants high prices for goods that came from far away. In Europe, the goods were sold for an even higher price. Still, Italian traders sold a lot and became very rich.

Traders in other countries watched Italian merchants and began to get an idea.

"What if we went to those faraway places ourselves?" they thought. "We could bring the goods for a lower price and still make a big profit!" They had to solve many problems before they reached their goal. They were not sure how to reach those places. They did not even have ships for the journey. In the next section, you will find out how the problems were solved.

Understanding Section 2:

1. Who is Marco Polo and why is he important?
2. How had Europeans already known about goods from China?
3. What are the continents of the Old World? Where is Europe?
4. Why had Europeans been afraid to trade and travel long ago?
5. (a) Where was the center of trade in the Old World?
   (b) Name some of the goods traded in the bazaars, and tell how they came to these markets.
6. Name the first Italian city which traded with Muslim lands.
7. Why did the kings and the Pope send armies to the Muslim lands?
8. What made the Europeans want more trade goods from those lands?
9. Why do merchants charge a higher price for the goods they sell?
10. What new idea did the other European traders get?

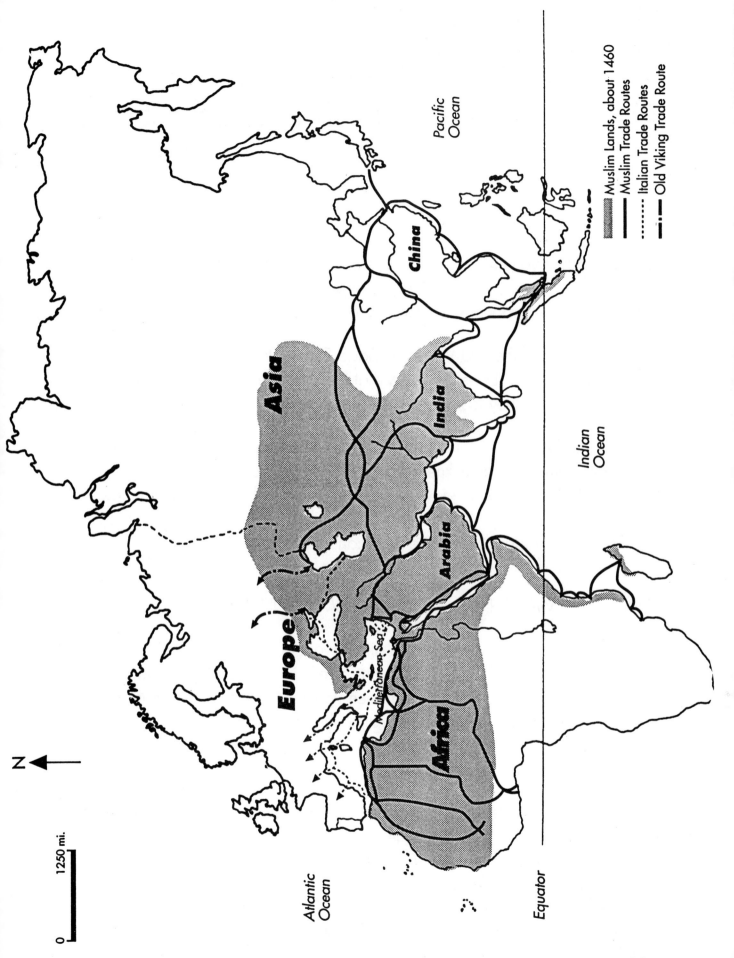

N

1250 mi.

0

Atlantic
Ocean

Europe

Mediterranean Sea

Africa

Arabia

Asia

India

China

Pacific
Ocean

Indian
Ocean

Equator

Muslim Lands, about 1460

Muslim Trade Routes

Italian Trade Routes

Old Viking Trade Route

Why Did Europeans Want to Find an All-water Route to the East?

When you think about explorers, you might picture wooden ships with sails, and cannons sticking out of their sides. Do you know why Europeans wanted to cross the oceans to reach the East?

Look at the map of the Old World on page 22. Try to find the shortest route from Europe to India. Doesn't it show that the shortest way to the East is across land? Why didn't they journey to the East by land?

As you read, Muslim leaders and their armies ruled and protected these lands. Merchants from these lands knew the routes and controlled the trade. Besides, Muslim traders already traded with Europe. There were Italian traders in every city. Certainly Muslim merchants would trade with other countries, too. Merchants trade with anyone who can pay for their goods.

EUROPEANS WANTED TO BYPASS MUSLIM TRADERS

First, remember that these Europeans didn't want to buy goods from Muslim merchants anymore. They wanted to buy directly from India and China. The Church and the kings of Europe had been fighting Muslims in their home lands. Europeans admired Muslims' cities, their scientific knowledge and many other things about the Muslims' way of life. Europeans also wanted to spread the Christian religion.

Europeans knew that Islam was very powerful and growing. Muslim merchants had traded in the East for a long time. They knew the best routes and the best places to get goods. Eastern people were used to trading with Muslims. Islam was spreading among the people in those lands. It would not be easy to take this trade away from the Muslims and spread Christianity in those lands. The Europeans knew they would have to find another route to the East.

PRINCE HENRY OF PORTUGAL LOOKED TO THE SEA

The armies that went to capture Jerusalem had lost. In Spain and Portugal, Christian armies were winning. They fought to push the Muslims back into North Africa. Prince Henry, son of the king of Portugal, was a soldier in these battles. He wanted to make his country great and powerful. He would find an all-water route to the East! His plan was to push out into the ocean, go around the Muslim lands, and take control of the trade for Portugal. They could trade with the East and spread the Christian religion.

Understanding Section 3:

1. The shortest route to India from Europe went through whose lands?
2. Why didn't Europeans want to buy goods from Muslim merchants anymore?
3. For what two reasons did Europeans want to go to the East?
4. Why was it difficult for the Christians to carry out their idea of going to the East?
5. Who was Prince Henry and what was his plan?

Muslim astronomers studied the stars from observatories like this one. These carefully placed platforms helped astronomers make accurate measurements of the movement of stars and planets. These astronomers developed mathematics and instruments that helped people pray towards Makkah, sail the seas on long journeys, measure the size of the earth and begin to understand our universe. Without their work, modern people may never have made it to the moon!

32

How Did Henry the Navigator Carry out his Plan?

How could Henry find an all-water route? For Europeans, the seas were unknown, horrible and full of monsters. Anyone foolish enough to sail out in the oceans would die. They imagined the people of faraway lands as we think of people from outer space. Europeans had little idea about the lands on the way to Asia. Their sailors weren't even sure if an all-water route could be found. Henry planned to conquer those fears. For his time, Henry's plan was like going to another galaxy today. They would need to study and learn much before they could reach their goal.

HENRY KNEW WHERE KNOWLEDGE COULD BE FOUND

Henry knew that Muslims had much knowledge about ships and sailing the seas. They knew about geography. Travelers had kept careful records of their many journeys. Pilgrims to Makkah, like Ibn Jubair, wrote books about their travels. Al-Masudi and Al-Biruni were Muslim geographers and scientists who wrote books about faraway places. Al-Masudi even described the Atlantic Ocean and some of its islands. Ibn Battuta of Morocco wrote about his wide travels by land and sea.

Henry had surely seen accurate maps like ones made by Al-Idrisi, who worked for the King of Sicily. Muslim pilots and sea-captains knew about storms and dangerous places along their routes. This information was written in books by Sulaiman Tajir, Ibn Majid and others.

Henry knew about tools Muslim navigators used to find their way far from land. They used an **astrolabe** to measure their position by the sun and stars. Even when storm-clouds hid the sky, they could find direction with a compass. A compass is a magnetized needle that always points north.

Henry must have heard about the fast, strong ships used by Muslim traders to carry heavy loads. He had seen them in Muslim Spain and North Africa. He heard stories about ships in waters Europeans had never seen. He might have heard about Moroccans sailing far out into the ocean. He heard about rich African kingdoms far to the South.

Most of all, Henry heard about Muslims trading in the East. Trading ships sailed from Africa's east coast to the gates of the Pacific Ocean. They stopped at ports from Africa all the way to China. Cloth, metals, jewels, medicines and perfumes, woods and animal products were traded peacefully among people of many lands. Sometimes Muslims were captains of large Chinese boats. Hindus, Muslims and Buddhists traded together in rich Asian kingdoms.

PRINCE HENRY GATHERED MANY SCIENTISTS AND SAILORS

Prince Henry left the easy life in his father's palace. He went to his castle at Sagres, a windy place on the coast of Portugal. There he started a school of navigation (or directing a ship). He brought together knowledge about **navigation** from the world of his day. He used it to help find a new route to Asia from Europe. Henry was later called "The Navigator" for his work.

Henry brought scientists and map-makers, geographers, sailors and ship-builders to his school. Traders and sea captains came. Muslim prisoners of war traded their knowledge for their freedom. Others hoped to gain money or land. Adventurers came, dreaming of great riches. Some were scholars who just wanted to learn and share knowledge. Many of those at Henry's sea-side castle knew how to read Arabic. Others were brought to translate Arabic into Latin.

HENRY'S SHIPS FOUND HARDSHIPS ON THE OPEN SEAS

What was it like to sail in those days? Out on the open sea, there were no hills, towns or harbors to tell a captain where he was. There were only deep salt water and waves as far as he could see. The ship had to carry all drinking-water needed for the crew, or collect it from rainwater. The ship had to carry most food needed for the journey. It needed to be dried or salted so it wouldn't spoil. As journeys became longer, the sailors found out that food

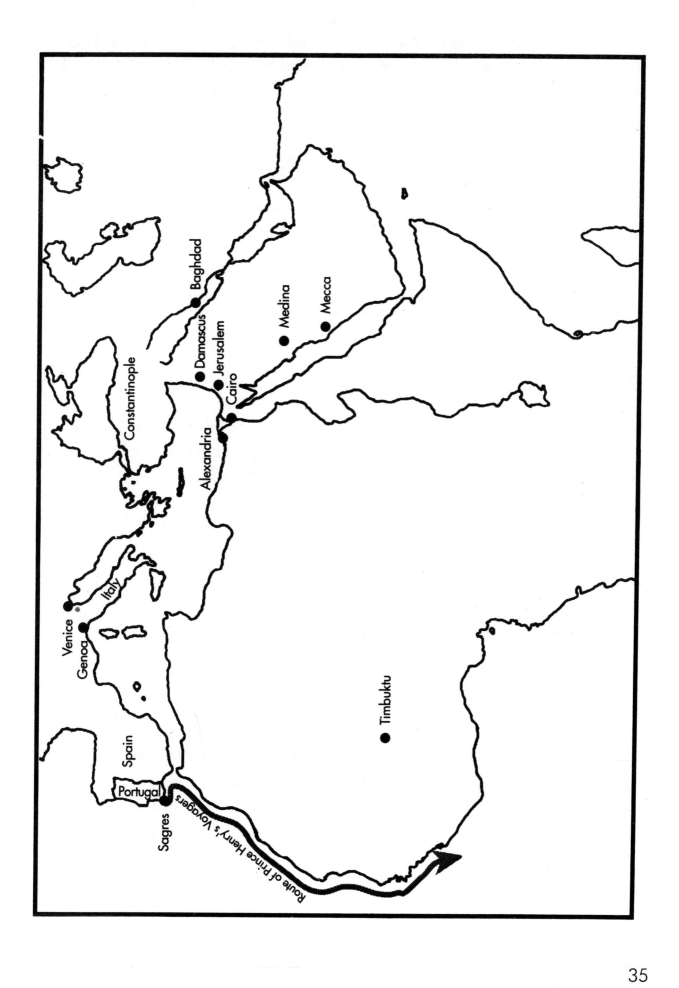

Baghdad

Medina

Mecca

Damascus

Jerusalem

Constantinople

Cairo

Alexandria

Italy

Venice

Genoa

Timbuktu

Spain

Portugal

Sagres

Route of Prince Henry's Voyagers

and water were not enough. If the crew did not eat fresh fruit for a long time, they became ill with **scurvy**. Scurvy was caused by lack of Vitamin C. It took many years before sailors learned to take limes and lemons on voyages.

The most difficult problem was getting anywhere at all! Without motors, ships moved only by catching the wind's power in sails. The wind didn't always blow in the direction the captain wanted to go. Sometimes it blew too much. Storms could break a ship into pieces. Sometimes wind didn't blow at all. The crew could die if their supplies ran out before the wind came up.

Before Henry's time, ships in Europe sailed along the coasts from port to port. They stayed within sight of land. Ships were heavy, small and slow. They could never make the long journey to Asia.

EXPLORERS NEED A NEW KIND OF SHIP

Henry sent ships out to explore the coast of Africa. They felt their way into the unknown. After many voyages, they saw the need for a better kind of ship. They were going out into the open ocean for the first time.

They needed to invent a ship for exploration. This ship must be able to do many different things. It had to be:

• strong enough to face the winds and waves of the deep ocean.

• large enough to carry all the supplies and cargo for a long voyage.

• small enough to sail near the coasts and into rivers to explore new lands.

• easy for a small crew to sail, even if some men became ill.

Inventors have always looked at good ideas from the past and tried to fit the best ones together into their new inventions. The shipbuilders at Henry's school did the same. Let us look at some of the ships from which they borrowed parts.

VIKING SHIP

EUROPEAN INVENTORS LOOK TO VIKINGS AND ARABS FOR IDEAS

Both Europeans and Arabs knew the strong, speedy ships of the Vikings. They were master sailors and shipbuilders. They sailed all over the northern Atlantic Ocean and down the rivers of Europe. The picture shows how their ships were built of wooden strips, called **planks**. Planks were nailed together so they overlapped like "clinkers" on a house's roof. "Clinker-built" ships were strong. They sailed well in rough northern waters. Viking ships had one large, square sail. Men rowed the ships with long, wooden paddles called **oars**. A square sail was very good if the wind was behind the ship. However, square sails could not catch the wind from any other direction.

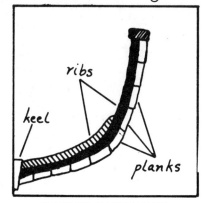

CARVEL-BUILT HULL

Later Europeans copied the Viking ships, changing them to carry more cargo for trade. These ships, called **cogs**, were fine for sailing near the coast. **Cogs** were not good for long voyages on the open sea. Cogs were still seen in Henry's time.

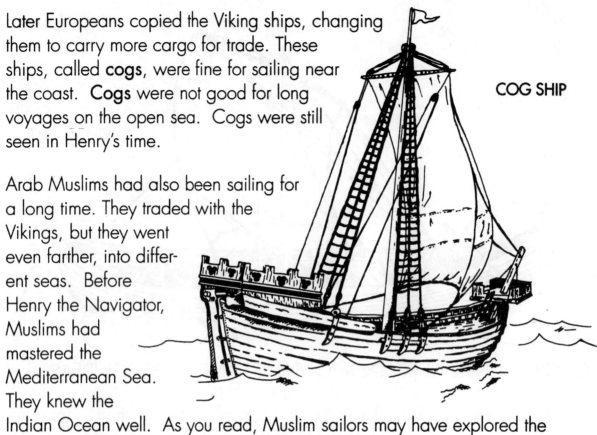

COG SHIP

Arab Muslims had also been sailing for a long time. They traded with the Vikings, but they went even farther, into different seas. Before Henry the Navigator, Muslims had mastered the Mediterranean Sea. They knew the Indian Ocean well. As you read, Muslim sailors may have explored the African coast and some of the Atlantic Ocean.

In the Mediterranean, Arabs used ships held together with iron nails. In the Indian Ocean, their ships were built in a different way. They were "sewn" together with ropes passed through holes in the hard tropical wood. The holes were closed with arabic gum. The wood was oiled to protect it from salt water and insects. A sewn ship lasted about 60 years. The iron on ships held together with nails lasted only 10 years.

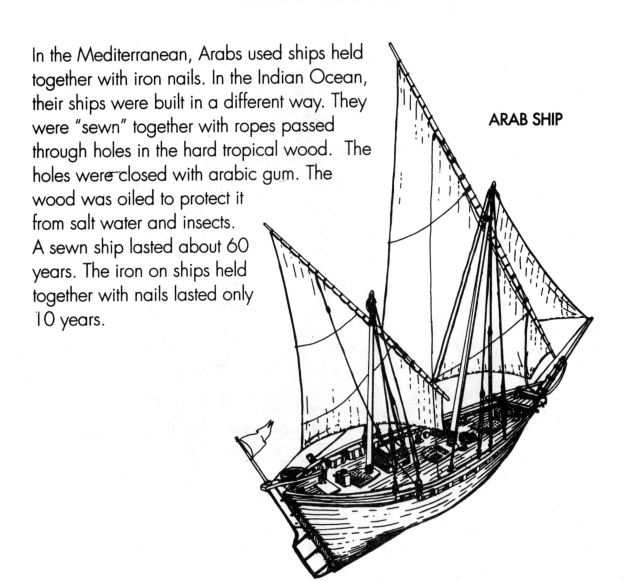

ARAB SHIP

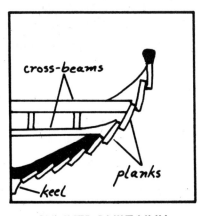

cross-beams

planks

keel

CLINKER-BUILT HULL

The **hull** (floating sides and bottom) of Arab ships was "carvel-built." Planks were placed next to each other without overlapping. This made the hull smooth on the outside. It also made the ship strong and light. The seams could stretch and move. Rough seas might snap a nailed ship into pieces.

Two or three triangular sails made Arab ships fast. Triangular sails catch the wind from almost any direction. This kind of ship was used in the days when the "Sindbad" stories were first told. Fishermen and traders near the Persian Gulf use boats almost like them today. This ship is called a **dhow**.

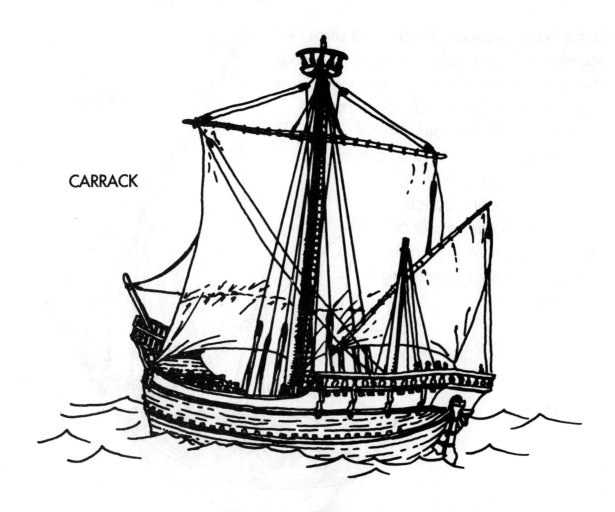

CARRACK

SHIPBUILDERS BORROW IDEAS TO MAKE THE CARAVEL

Henry's shipbuilders borrowed the smooth hull from Arab ships. They also borrowed triangular sails. Some ships in the Mediterranean, called **carracks**, already used these ideas. As Henry's sailors explored farther down the coast of Africa, they made more changes in the ships.

CARAVEL

The result was a new kind of ship, called the caravel. It looked much like Arab ships from the Indian Ocean. It was nailed together, and had three large triangular sails. It was larger, but also light, easy to handle and fast. It was good in any weather, and perfect for exploring the coastline. After Henry's death, explorers stopped sailing close to the African coastline on their way South. They began to sail out into the open sea.

The Portuguese continued to improve ships, making them faster, larger and more comfortable. They added square sails to triangular sails. They added cannons fired from holes in the hull.

Christopher Columbus took three ships to the New World. One of these was a caravel. The other two were the newer kind with many sails and cannons. You can see a picture one of these on page 35. Count the sails on his ship!

You can see a picture one of these on page 35.

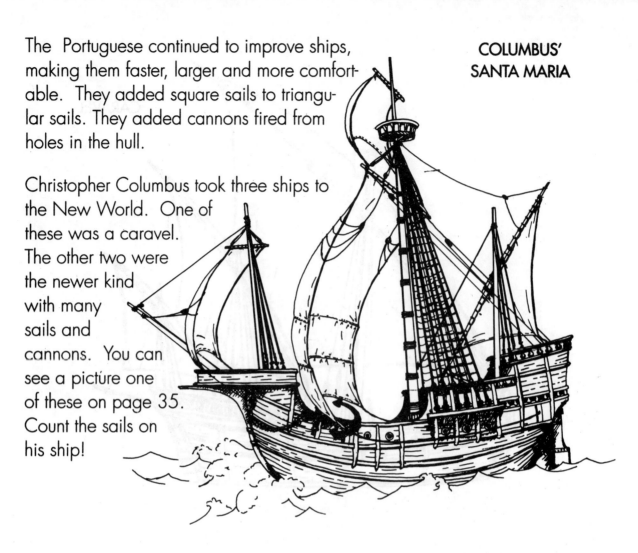

COLUMBUS' SANTA MARIA

Understanding Section 4:

1. What was Prince Henry's first step in carrying out his plan to find an all-water route to the East?
2. Name two groups which had much knowledge about navigation in those days.
3. What kind of people did Henry need to help him gather information about navigation?
4. Name two difficulties in sailing on the open sea.
5. Why did Henry and his explorers need a new kind of ship?
6. Describe the Viking ships in one sentence.
7. Describe the ship used by the Arabs in the Indian Ocean.
8. Why is a triangular sail better than a square sail?
9. What ideas did Henry's shipbuilders borrow?
10. In what kind of ships did Columbus sail to the New World?

Why Did Columbus Want to Reach the East by Sailing West?

During Henry's lifetime, Europeans did not reach Asia by sea. They only reached a short distance down the African coast. The map on page 28 shows the route of Henry's ships. After Henry's death, exploration continued. The Portuguese explorer Vasco Da Gama reached India by an all-water route in 1497.

Columbus sailed west in 1492. It seems strange that Columbus wanted to sail in the opposite direction. The Portuguese had not yet found the route. There are good reasons for Columbus' journey in the "wrong" direction.

COLUMBUS PROMISED TO CLAIM LANDS AND RICHES

To understand, we must go back to the Church and its leader, the Pope. The Pope had found out about Henry's plans, and he was very pleased. He hoped that Henry's work would help the Christians. To reward him, he wrote an order to all the Christian kings in Europe. The Pope said that any lands or people Henry's sailors found would be Portugal's forever. King Ferdinand and Queen Isabella of Spain paid for Columbus' voyage. Since they belonged to the Church, they had to obey the Pope.

Columbus gave Spain a chance to get rich without disobeying the Church. He told them he could reach the East by sailing west. He would claim these lands for Spain, and fill the ships with spices, silk and other goods. He made the king and queen believe his route was shorter than Portugal's.

Columbus made a mistake. He didn't realize how big the world was. He didn't know that North and South America lay on the way to the East. Columbus' mistakes made Spain the richest country in Europe for a time!

Understanding Section 5:

1. Did the Portuguese find an all-water route to Asia before Henry died?
2. Who was the first European to reach India by an all-water route?
3. How did the Pope reward Henry the Navigator for his work?
4. Who paid for Columbus' voyage? What was the name of their country?
5. What did Columbus promise King Ferdinand and Queen Isabella?
6. What were Columbus' two big mistakes?

1. **legends** = stories which are part truth and part invention
2. **scholars** = people who study to gain knowledge
3. **invaders**=groups of people who move into other lands with armies
4. **bazaars** = great, covered markets
5. **merchants** = traders who buy and sell goods
6. **trade routes** = roads or ways traders use to carry goods
7. **profit** = the money that a merchant earns for himself
8. **navigation** = directing ships travelling on the seas
9. **compass** = a magnetized needle that always points north
10. **scurvy** = an illness suffered on long sailing voyages
11. **planks** = wooden strips used to build the body of a ship
12. **oars** = long wooden paddles used to move a ship
13. **hull** = floating sides and bottom of a ship

PEOPLE TO REMEMBER

Christopher Columbus
Marco Polo
Henry the Navigator
The Pope
King Ferdinand and Queen Isabella
Vasco Da Gama

Al-Masudi
Al-Biruni
Ibn Battuta
Al-Idrisi
Sulaiman Tajir
Ibn Majid
Ibn Jubair

PLACES TO REMEMBER

Mediterranean Sea
Atlantic Ocean
Indian Ocean
China
India
Spain
Portugal } Al-Andalus

Italy (Genoa & Venice)
Cairo
Alexandria
Bagdad
Damascus
Jerusalem

IDEAS TO REMEMBER

Islam - Muslims
Christianity - Christians
trade.
Old World
exploration
"clinker-built"
square sails
"carvel-built"
triangular sails

Arab ship - dhow
Viking ship
cog
carrack
caravel

Part III:

Teaching Suggestions & Enrichment Activities

PRE-READING:

1. Before beginning this unit, you may wish to discuss the many facts, legends and shreds of evidence on the subject of who actually discovered the Americas and when. These include Phoenecians, the so-called "Red-Paint People" of the Stone Age, the Atlantis legend, Africans, Chinese, Vikings, and a group of 9th century Irish monks. There is evidence in favor of each of these stories. Review the bibliography at the end of these notes for sources of information.

Note: Before each of the following sections, introduce new vocabulary, both boldface terms in the text and any other words unfamiliar to the students. This will enable the students to concentrate on the complex and numerous ideas in each séction.

SECTION 1: What did people know about the world in Columbus' time?

1. Develop a definition of the word **legend**. At this time, you may wish to discuss another type of legend with the students — that of **myths** about the shape of the world which have been held by ancient peoples. As a tie-in to science, students may be interested in exploring how scientists learned that the world is round.

2. Using classroom or desk maps, orient students to the location of the places mentioned in Section 1. (the Mediterranean Sea, Greece, the Arabian Peninsula, the Iberian Peninsula, Italy, and the Muslim lands) Ask the students what were the best ways to communicate and travel between those lands in the days before telephones and airplanes. (ships and land transport like walking or using animals)

3. Discuss with the students why people trade goods (to get things not found in their own land) and how people exchange ideas even across seas and mountains. Discuss what things make it easy to exchange ideas (same language, same religion, easy and safe travel) and what kinds of ideas travel quickly. (inventions that make life easier, written ideas that are easy to carry, beautiful and precious things , etc.) In this and following lessons, give the students background information on the cultural, technological and economic level attained by the Islamic civilization at that time, which was approximately 750 years after Hijrah, the migration of the Muslims to Medina, which marks the beginning of the Muslim calendar. The bibliography lists titles which contain this information. *Aramco World Magazine's* special one-author issue for the quincentennial of the Columbus voyage, "The Middle East and the Age of Discovery," (May-June 1992) provides a corrective to typical images of non-

European cultures as passive recipients of Western knowledge and power. The articles discuss everything from food origins to mapmaking and astronomy, such as the firm authority attributed by Columbus' contemporaries to the state of Muslim knowledge of astronomy and mathematics. If a teacher had time to consult only one source for enrichment, these articles would be a good choice.

SECTION 2: Why did Columbus want to travel to the East?

1. You may wish to expand upon the story of Marco Polo by means of a filmstrip, your textbook, or a student oral report.

2. Using a globe and a wall or desk map of the world, have students identify the continents of the "Old World," and discuss why the other continents were not included. (because they are separated from the others by oceans, and hence were unknown to Europeans) Going over the ideas in Section 2, contrast the isolation of Europe long ago with other civilizations in the Old World — China, India and the Muslim lands. Reinforce the text material on trade goods and the routes they travelled, using the map provided. Assign worksheets # 1 and # 2.

3. Discuss the competition between faiths. The mode of discussion will depend entirely upon the readiness and depth of information in individual groups. Apart from a free-wheeling debate about why people go to war over religious beliefs, it is important for later events that the students understand why the Pope was a figure of authority who could command obedience. Since it is so essential to the motivation of the Europeans to explore, and since it will appear later in conjunction with the natives of the "discovered" lands, the subject is introduced here in connection with the growth of trade through the Crusaders' exposure to new ideas. In addition, the subject of Christian victories in Al-Andalus is discussed in Section 3, since it was no accident that Henry the Navigator, whose motives were definitely related to his desire to defeat Islam and further the goals of Christianity, was from the Iberian Peninsula. As a note of information, the defeat of the Muslims in Granada, their last stronghold in Europe, took place in 1492, the same famous year of Columbus' voyage. It was the removal of that burden of warfare which released the money from Isabella and Ferdinand's treasury to fund the voyage which brought such fantastic riches to Spain.

4. In order to clarify the mechanics of trade, have the students name any product which comes to us from a foreign country. Trace the route this product takes, what could happen to it on the way, and what middlemen handle it on the way to the stores where we can buy it. Discuss how the price gets higher each time the product

changes hands. Ask the students whether they think they could get the product cheaper if they cut out all the middlemen and went to the foreign country to bring it. Ask whether someone could become rich by going to a far place to bring something which many people want to buy. Have them give some examples of goods like that. Explain why spices, medicines, perfumes, etc., were such products in those days. Discuss the idea of competition between traders, and show how the Spanish began to develop their big plan.

SECTION 3: Why did Europeans want an all-water route to the East?

1. Using a wall map and a yardstick or string, have students point out the shortest routes to India and China from Europe. Locate the geographic obstacles to easy travel over these routes (the students are certain to come up with some novel suggestions). Then discuss human obstacles to the possiblity that the Europeans would choose the short overland route to carry out their plans. It is important that the students realize that Europeans did not have maps like we have today. They did not know the shape of these lands or their inhabitants, and they knew only superstitious legends about many places.

SECTION 4: How did Henry the Navigator carry out his plan?

1. When the students have begun reading Section 4 about ships and sailing on the open seas, the class may begin the model project (see project instructions). Once supplies are passed out, directions have been given, and the students are at work, it may be possible to read aloud exerpts from one or more of the *Sindbad* stories for enrichment and atmosphere and to give the students an impression of the nature of long-distance trade. They contain many opportunities for pointing out concrete clues to the way of life of a merchant in those days.

2. Discuss how Henry the Navigator conceived and carried out his plan, and how others helped him. It is important to qualify the contribution of leaders especially in studying the Age of Exploration, which is chararacterized by heroes whose contributions are viewed as their own accomplishments. The work, knowledge and sacrifice of lesser players is often overlooked. Discussion may center around questions of what role leaders play in great events. Are they people with wealth and power? Do they possess special knowledge, or do they bring together people who do by having the means to reward them? In the case of Henry, it is important to note that in spite of his title, "Navigator," he never set foot on the exploring ships he sent out. Many lesser people lost their lives on these voyages. Discuss similar events in history where one individual

is given most of the credit for an accomplishment in which many participated. Discuss how historians and others need someone to "stand for" a big event as a hero. It is difficult to discover the other players, since they are not usually named. Draw the students' attention to the ways in which this issue has special importance for the Age of Exploration. Draw parallels to any kind of team effort, in which the captain, not the crew, gets credit; the team star or coach and not the others; the general and not the soldiers. The teacher may assign students to write about such an experience of their own.

3.   For reinforcement and enrichment, the filmstrip which accompanies this unit covers Section 4 and adds some detail to discussion of the ships. It also ties together some points in the other sections. If preferred, work through this section with students by using worksheet #4 to have them write a letter in which they imagine themselves on a ship living through a difficult voyage on the open sea. Trace the development of the ships as described in the text, comparing the illustrations and emphasizing the borrowing of elements from each. To reinforce and organize these ideas, use the chart in worksheet #5.

SECTION 5: Why did Columbus want to reach the East by sailing west?

1.   Using the text, explain the connection between the Pope's reward for Henry and Portugal and why Columbus chose to look for a different route. [Note: For the teacher's information and to provide documentation, the Papal Bull of 1454 is reproduced at the end of these notes.]

2.   Ask the students to look at the globe and imagine how large it would be if there were no more ocean surface, but North and South America were missing. Interesting with regard to measuring the circumference of the earth without benefit of satellites or circumnavigation is the fact that Greeks and Arabs, among other peoples, set themselves to measure a degree of longitude with remarkable accuracy.

3.   Close the discussion of this unit by noting the final sentence that Columbus' mistakes made Spain the wealthiest country in Europe for a time. This discussion will prepare students for specific information on Columbus' voyage and those of explorers who followed him during the Age of Exploration.

4.   Complete the worksheet packet, review vocabulary and learning objectives, and implement the included evaluation instrument or alternative.

DOCUMENT STUDY

The following is quoted from pages 30-31, Panikkar, *Asia and Western Dominance:*

In 1454 he [Prince Henry of Portugal] received from the Pope Nicholas V the right to all discoveries up to India. The Bull, which is of fundamental importance and is the first of three which determines the Portuguese monopoly in the East, is quoted below:

'Our joy is immense to know that our dear son, Henry, Prince of Portugal, following the footsteps of his father of illustrious memory, King John, inspired with a zeal for souls like an intrepid soldier of Christ, has carried into the most distant and unknown countries the name of God and has brought into the Catholic fold the perfidious enemies of God and Christ, such as the Saracens and the Infidels.

'After having established Christian families in some of the unoccupied islands of the Ocean and having consecrated churches there for the celebration of the Holy Mysteries the Prince, remembering that never within the memory of man had anyone been known to navigate the sea to the distant shores of the Orient, believed that he could give God best evidence of his submission, if by his effort the Ocean can be made navigable as far as India, which, it is said, is already subject to Christ. If he enters into relations with these people, he will induce them to come to the help of the Christians of the West against the enemies of the faith. At the same time, he will bring under submission, with the King's permission, the pagans of the countries not yet inflicted with the plague of Islam and give them knowledge of the name of Christ.

'It is thus that during the last twenty-five years that without the support of the armies of Portugal, but in the midst of the greatest trials, he in his fast caravels, searched without repose the meridianal regions to the Antarctic pole [sic] across the oceans, and after having traversed numerous seas reached at last the province of Guinea and from there pushed further to the mouth of the river commonly known as the Nile [sic].

'We, after careful deliberation, and having considered that we have by our apostolic letters conceded to King Affonso, the right, total and absolute, to invade, conquer and subject all the countries which are under the rule of the enemies of Christ, Saracen or Pagan, by our apostolic letter we wish the same King Affonso, the Prince, and all their successors, occupy and possess in exclusive rights the said islands, ports and the seas undermentioned, and all faithful Christians are prohibited without permission of the said Affonso and his successors to encroach on their sovereignty. Of the conquests already made, or to be made, all the conquests which extend to Cape Bojador and Cape Non to the coast of Guinea and all the Orient is perpetually and for the future the sovereignty of King Affonso.'

On March 13, 1456, Calixtus III promulgated a second Bull confirming the grant of Nicholas V. Thus Henry was able to obtain what in the 15th century was an absolute and incontestable title and, further, to proclaim both the political and religious objects of his work. The one thing that stands out most clearly in the Papal Bull, and which was to influence policy for a hundred years to come, was the combination of the spiritual urge to conquer heathen lands for Christ with the fanatical zeal to cut at the root of Islam by attacking it from behind.

The next stage in the mission of Portugal was the Treaty of Trodesilhas signed on June 9, 1494. By this treaty Portugal and Spain fixed a line 370 leagues west of Cape Verde Islands as the demarcation of their respective zones.

Asia and Western Dominance. K. M. Panikkar. London: Allen & Unwin, 1953.

The Adventures of Ibn Battuta: A Muslim Traveler of the 14th Century. Ross E. Dunn. Berkeley and L.A.: University of California Press, 1986.

The Arab Navigation. Sulaiman Nadvi. Lahore: Sh. Muhammad

Explorers and Explorations. Eric Protter. New York: Grosset & Dunlap, 1962.

Fusang: The Chinese Who Built America. Stan Steiner. New York: Harper & Row, 1979.

The First Ships 'Round the World. Walter Brownlee. Cambridge: Cambridge University Press, 1974. (A topic book from the series *Cambridge Introduction to the History of Mankind*, Trevor Cairns, editor.)

A History of Islamic Spain. W. Mongomery Watt. Edinburgh: Edinburgh University Press, 1965.

A History of Moorish Spain. Richard Fletcher. New York: Henry Holt & Company, 1992.

"In the Wake of Sindbad," Tim Severin, *National Geographic*, July 1982.

"The Middle East and the Age of Discovery," Paul Lunde, *Aramco World Magazine*, May-June 1992.

Muslim Contribution to Geography. Nafis Ahmad. New Delhi: Adam Publishers, 1945, 1982.

Medieval Cities. Henri Pirenne. Princeton: Princeton University Press, 1925.

The Oxford Illustrated History of Medieval Europe. George Holmes, ed.. Oxford: Oxford University Press, 1988.

"Prince Henry, the Explorer Who Stayed Home," Alan Villiers, *National Geographic*, November 1960.

"Secrets of the Lost Red-Paint People," NOVA/ PBS Television Series. Boston: WGBH Television, 1987.

Travellers and Explorers, IQRA Foundation, 1992.

The Venture of Islam: Conscience and History in a World Civilization (Vol. 1-3). Marshall G.S. Hodgson. Chicago and London: University of Chicago Press, 1974.

The Viking Ships. Ian Atkinson. Cambridge: Cambridge University Press, 1979. (A topic book from the series Cambridge Introduction to the History of Mankind , Trevor Cairns, editor)

"Vinland Ruins Prove Vikings Found the New World," Helga Ingstad, *National Geographic*, November 1964.

"The Voyage of 'Brendan'," Timothy Severin, *National Geographic*, November 1977.

"Who Discovered America? A New Look At an Old Question," editor, *National Geographic*, December 1977.

ILLUSTRATIONS

The ship illustrations are adapted from Graham Humphrey's drawings in *The First Ships 'round the World*, with the exception of the Viking ship, which is from archaeological reconstructions pictured in *The Viking Ships*, and the Arab ship, which is adapted from a diagram of the **Sohar** in Tim Severin's account of his reconstructed voyage in the *National Geographic Magazine*, July 1982.

Section 1:
1. How did people long ago learn that the world is round?
2. What did the Muslim scientists do with the knowledge gained in their new lands?
3. How do traders help to spread ideas?
4. How did the Muslims' scientific knowledge come to Europe?
5. Why was Italy an important trading country?

Key
1. They studied the stars and planets to prove that it is round.
2. They translated the old books into Arabic, and used the knowledge to build new discoveries.
3. They see inventions and hear about scientific discoveries in lands where they trade. Then they return to their countries and tell about it.
4. Europeans had the Arabic books translated into their languages, and Italian traders brought the ideas with their goods.
5. Italy sticks out into the Mediterranean Sea like a boot, so it has a long coastline for ships.

Section 2:
1. Who is Marco Polo and why is he important?
2. How had Europeans already known about goods from China?
3. What are the continents of the Old World? Where is Europe?
4. Why had Europeans been afraid to trade and travel long ago?
5. (a)Where was the center of trade in the Old World?
    (b)Name some of the goods traded in the bazaars, and tell how they came to these markets.
6. Name the first Italian city which traded with the Muslim lands.
7. Why did the kings and the Pope send armies to the Muslim lands?
8. What made the Europeans want more trade goods from those lands?
9. Why do merchants charge a higher price for the goods they sell?
10. What new idea did the other European traders get?

Key
1. He wrote a book about his travels to China. This book made Europeans interested in trade with China.
2. They had seen and admired the goods in Muslim Spain, and Italian traders brought them to Europe to sell.
3. They are Europe, Asia and Africa. Europe is on the western edge.
4. They were afraid of invaders, so they lived in castles and made or grew everything they needed.
5. (a)The great cities of the Muslim lands (Cairo, Bagdad and Damascus) were the centers of trade
    (b) answers vary
6. Venice was the first Italian city which traded with Muslim lands.
7. They believed it was their duty to God to fight the Muslims. They wanted to take over their lands and make them Christian.
8. The soldiers saw a better way of life while they were in the Muslim lands.They took home stories and samples of the goods.
9. They have to pay for the goods, for transportation, and for goods they might lose on the way to market.
10. They wanted to go to faraway lands themselves to bring goods and make a bigger profit.

Section 3:
1. The shortest route to India from Europe went through whose lands?
2. Why didn"t the Europeans want to buy goods from the Muslim merchants anymore?
3. For what two reasons did Europeans want to go to the East?
4. Why was it difficult for the Christians to carry out their idea of going to the East?
5. Who was Prince Henry and what was his plan?

Key

1. The shortest route went through the Muslim lands.
2. They wanted to bring the goods from the East by themselves.
3. They wanted to bring trade goods and spread Christianity to the people of the East.
4. The Muslims knew the best routes and the best places to get the goods, and the people were used to trading with them.
5. He was the son of the king of Portugal. His plan was to look for an all-water route to the East.

Section 4:

1. What was Prince Henry's first step in carrying out his plan to find an all-water route to the East?
2. Name two groups which had much knowledge about navigation in hose days?
3. What kind of people did Henry need to help him gather information about navigation?
4. Name two difficulties in sailing on the open sea.
5. Why did Henry and his explorers need a new kind of ship?
6. Describe the Viking ships in one sentence.
7. Describe the ship used by the Arabs in the Indian Ocean.
8. Why is a triangular sail better than a square sail?
9. What ideas did Henry's shipbuilders borrow?
10. In what kind of ships did Columbus sail to the New World?

Key

1. He left his father's palace and started a school of navigation.
2. The Muslim Arabs and the Vikings had much experience in navigation.
3. He needed geographers, map-makers, shipbuilders, sailors and scientists.
4. Answers vary.
5. Their ships were too heavy, small, and slow to make the long journey to Asia. They could not sail on the open ocean.
6. The Viking ships were "clinker-built" of wood, with one square sail and had many men with oars.
7. The Arab ships had a smooth, "carvel-built" hull which was sewn together with ropes, and used two or three triangular sails.
8. A triangular sail can be turned to catch the wind from many different directions.
9. They borrowed the idea of the smooth hull and the triangular sails.
10. He had three ships — a caravel, and two of the new ships with many sails and cannon.

Section 5:

1. Did the Portugese find an all-water route to Asia before Henry died?
2. Who was the first European to reach India by an all-water route?
3. What did the Pope do to reward Henry the Navigator for his work?
4. Who paid for Columbus' voyage? What was the name of their country?
5. What did Columbus tell the king and queen that he could do for their country?
6. What were Columbus' two big mistakes?

Key

1. No, he died before they reached his goal.
2. Vasco Da Gama sailed to India in 1498.
3. He gave all the lands on the sailors ' route to Henry and his sons.
4. King Ferdinand and Queen Isabella of Spain paid for the voyage.
5. He told them that he could get to Asia in the East by sailing west. He promised them riches and lands.
6. He thought that the world was much smaller than it is. He also didn't know that North and South America block the way to Asia.

Name _____ WORKSHEET #1

Identify the following places on the map facing this page. Try to work from memory, but use the map on page __ of your student booklet for help.

1. Which three continents belong to the Old World? **Asia**

Africa   **Europe**

Label them in large letters on the map.

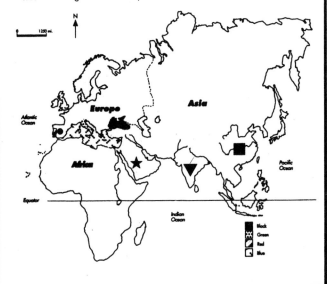

Name _____ WORKSHEET #2

The merchants' goods are for sale in the shops of the bazaar. Identify them, then match them up. Draw lines to connect the goods with the kind of transportation used to carry them, and the part of the old world where they came from.

Furs

Honey

Cotton

Salt

Pearls
Jewels

Drugs
Spices

Gold

Silk

Perfume
Incense

Silk, Pearls, Jewels,
Spices, Perfume, Cotton

Silk, Drugs, Cotton

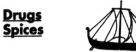
Honey, Furs, Wax

Salt, Gold, Silk,
Incense, Jewels, Pearls

RUSSIA
Honey
Furs

CHINA
Silk
Drugs

AFRICA
Gold
Salt

ARABIAN
PENINSULA
Incense
Pearls

INDIA and
the ASIAN
ISLANDS
Spices
Drugs
Cotton
Jewels
Perfume

Name _____ WORKSHEET #3

Fill in the vocabulary words from your student booklet to load up the ship with cargo to sail away.

DOWN
1. a magnetized needle that always points north
2. representatives of a foreign government
3. floating sides and body of a ship
4. the money that a merchant earns for himself
5. long, wooden paddles used to move a ship
6. great, covered market

ACROSS
4. wooden strips used to build the body of a ship
7. people who study to gain knowledge
8. traders who buy and sell goods
9. an illness suffered on long sailing voyages
10. directing a ship on the sea
11. stories which are part truth and part invention
12. roads or ways used by traders to carry goods
13. people who move into other lands with armies

Name _____ WORKSHEET #5

TYPES OF SHIPS

Fill in the chart below to show how the inventors got ideas to build the new ships for exploration. Use your text, pages 32-38 to help you.

	Hull	Sails	Number of sails
Viking Ships	rough, "clinker-built"	**square**	**1**
Arab Ships	**smooth, "carvel-**	triangular	**2**
Explorers' caravel	**smooth, "carvel-**	**triangular**	2 or 3
Columbus' Santa Maria	smooth, "carvel-built"	**square and triangular**	**4**

57

TRADERS AND EXPLORERS IN WOODEN SHIPS

Part A

1. f
2. b
3. g
4. h
5. e
6. a
7. d
8. c
9. i
10. j

Part B

11. Europe, Africa, Asia
12. Venice
13. silk, spices, gold, etc.
14. ship-builders, map-makers, geographers, etc.
15. Africa

Part C

16. c
17. b
18. c
19. b
20. a

Part D

1. B,C,F
2. B,C,F
3. A,D,E
4. A,B,C,G

Part IV:

Unit Activities

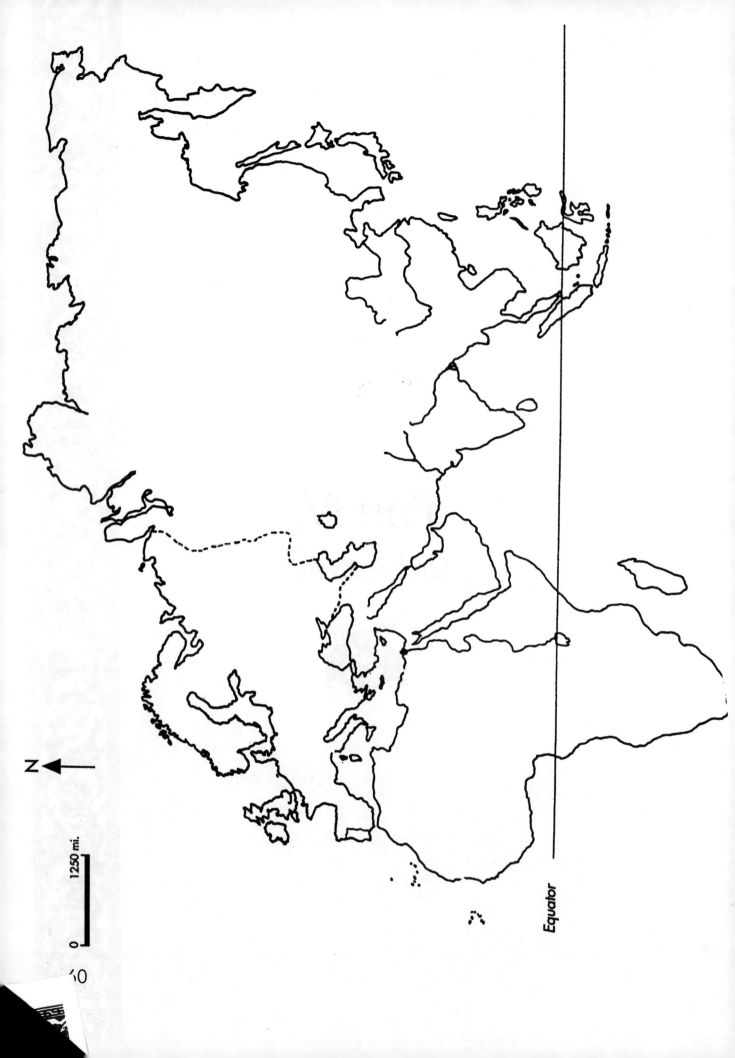

N

1250 mi.

0

Equator

Identify the following places on the map facing this page. Try to work from memory, but use the map on page 14 of your student booklet for help.

1. Which three continents belong to the Old World? _____

_____ _____

Label them in large letters on the map.

2. Label the Atlantic Ocean, the Indian Ocean, and the Pacific Ocean.

3. Color the Mediterranean Sea blue.

4. Put a ● in Spain.

5. Color Portugal red.

6. Put a ★ on the Arabian Peninsula.

7. Put a ▼ in India.

8. Put a ■ in China.

9. Color Italy green.

10. Color the Black Sea in black.

The merchants' goods are for sale in the shops of the bazaar. Identify them, then match them up. Draw lines to connect the goods with the kind of transportation used to carry them, and the part of the old world where they came from.

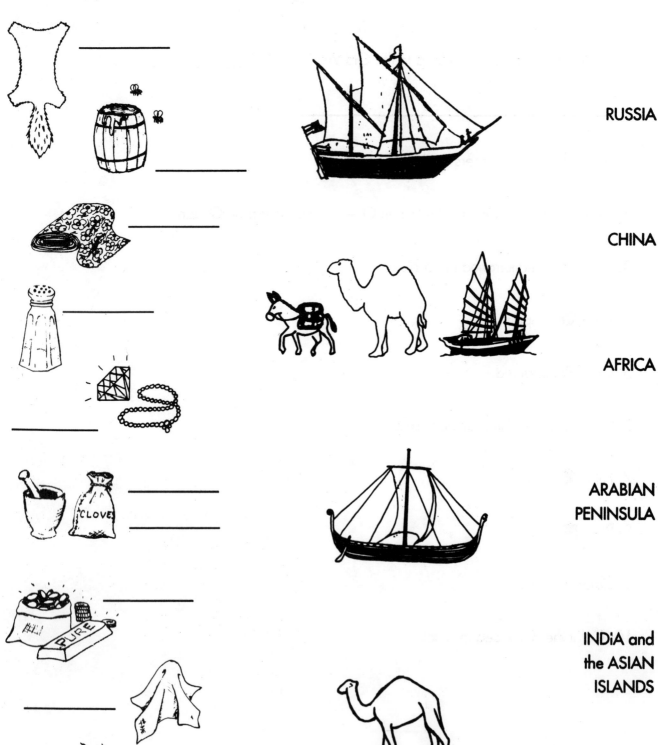

RUSSIA

CHINA

AFRICA

ARABIAN
PENINSULA

INDiA and
the ASIAN
ISLANDS

Fill in the vocabulary words from your student booklet to load up the ship with cargo to sail away.

DOWN

1. a magnetized needle that always points north
2. representatives of a foreign government
3. floating sides and body of a ship
4. the money that a merchant earns for himself
5. long, wooden paddles used to move a ship
6. great, covered market

ACROSS

4. wooden strips used to build the body of a ship
7. people who study to gain knowledge
8. traders who buy and sell goods
9. an illness suffered on long sailing voyages
10. directing a ship on the sea
11. stories which are part truth and part invention
12. roads or ways used by traders to carry goods
13. people who move into other lands with armies

Name WORKSHEET #4

You are a sailor on an explorer's ship. You have been at sea for two months. Write a letter home, describing your voyage and your life on board the ship.

TYPES OF SHIPS

Fill in the chart below to show how the inventors got ideas to build the new ships for exploration. Use your text, pages 32-38 to help you.

	Hull	Sails	Number of sails
Viking Ships	rough, "clinker-built"		
Arab Ships		triangular	
Explorers' caravel			2 or 3
Columbus' Santa Maria	smooth, "carvel-built"		

Name_____

Part A: Match the words below with their correct meaning. Write the letter of the word in front of its meaning.

a. hull	f. merchants
b. compass	g. navigation
c. legends	h. planks
d. scholars	i. trade routes
e. bazaars	j. profit

_____ 1. traders who buy and sell goods

_____ 2. a magnetized needle that always points north

_____ 3. directing ships travelling on the seas

_____ 4. wooden strips used to build the body of a ship

_____ 5. great, covered markets

_____ 6. floating sides and bottom of a ship

_____ 7. people who study to gain knowledge

_____ 8. stories which are part truth and part invention

_____ 9. roads or ways traders use to carry goods

_____ 10. the money that a merchant earns for himself

Part B: Fill in the blanks to complete the following sentences.

11. Name the three continents of the Old World. _____,

    _____, _____

12. Name the first city in Europe which traded with Muslim merchants.

    _____

13. List three trade goods brought by Muslim merchants from faraway lands.

    _____, _____, and _____

14. Name two kinds of scholars whom Prince Henry brought together to help him carry out his plan.

    _____

15. To get to the East, the Europeans had to sail around which continent?

    _____

Part C: Choose the answer which best completes the sentence and circle it.

16. Scientific knowledge was brought to Europe from Muslim lands
    a. by traders
    b. by translating books
    c. both a and b

17. Italy is an ideal country for trade because it
    a. is in a desert
    b. sticks out into the sea
    c. has many mountains

18. Al-Andalus was the Muslims' name for which lands?
    a. India and China
    b. Africa and Arabia
    c. Spain and Portugal

19. Europeans wanted to buy more trade goods from the East because
    a. they had all they needed in their own lands
    b. they had seen samples and heard about rich goods
    c. their armies had won many battles in the East

20. Prince Henry wanted to look for an all-water route to the East
    a. to take over the trade and spread Christianity
    b. to help shipbuilders make a new kind of ship
    c. to prove that the world is round

Part D: Match the parts below with the kind of ship to which they belong. Write the letter of the part in the blank in front of the correct ship.

A. square sail   E. 1 sail

B. triangular sails   F. 2 or 3 sails

C. "carvel-built" hull   G. 3 or more sails

D. "clinker-built" hull

1. Arab ships _____ _____ _____

2. Explorers' Caravel _____ _____ _____

3. Viking ships _____ _____ _____

4. Two of Columbus' ships (the Santa Maria)_____ _____ _____ _____

Time: Approximately 2-3 class periods, depending on class size.

Materials:

1 one-gallon plastic milk jug per ship

5-6 sheets 8 1/2" x 11" tagboard, preferably brown

2-3 sheets " " " white typing paper

    (equivalent amount of cloth for sails optional)

2-3 long wooden meat skewers (or equivalent 1-foot dowels)

small lump of plasticine or kitchen clay to secure masts

1-2 feet light packing string or strong thread

sharp pencils

markers or crayons

white glue

staplers (at least 1 for every 3 students)

scissors

mat knife (for the teacher only!)

Preparation:

1. Have each student bring in at least 1 milk jug (It is nice to have spares, but in a pinch the half with the handle also works.) Before the project can begin, the teacher will cut off the neck of the jug and cut it in half, as shown.

2. You may wish to cut the tagboard lengthwise in 3/4" strips with a paper cutter to save time and frustration.

NOTE: *Leave one sheet of tagboard per student whole for "decks"!*

3. With a photocopied instruction booklet for each pair, the students should fare well with a little assistance.

4. Follow directions. NOTE: In Step # 11, you may substitute a lump of plasticine or other clay to anchor the masts.

5. Bon Voyage!

**Project illustrations by Andrea Thigpen

1.

Carefully, cut === plastic jug in half.

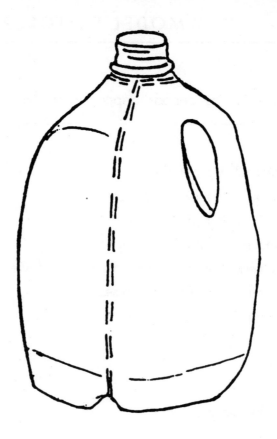

2.

Loosely, staple the keel to the front and back of the jug.

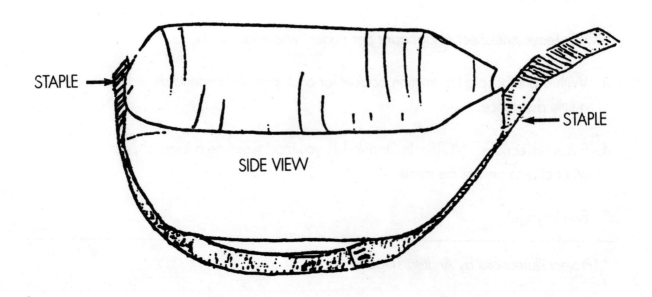

STAPLE →

→ STAPLE

SIDE VIEW

3.

— Staple 3 ribs (1, 2, 3) to the keel and sides of the ship.

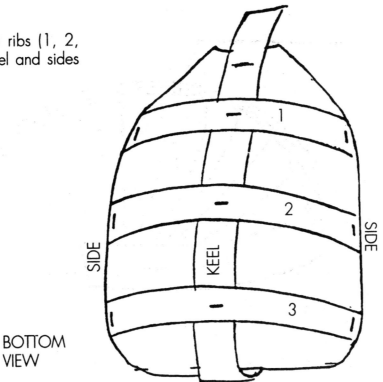

SIDE

KEEL

SIDE

1

2

3

BOTTOM VIEW

4.

(approx. 8-9 strips)

*Glue and staple strips across ribs. Start with rib 1, stop with rib 3.

*Glue is optional.

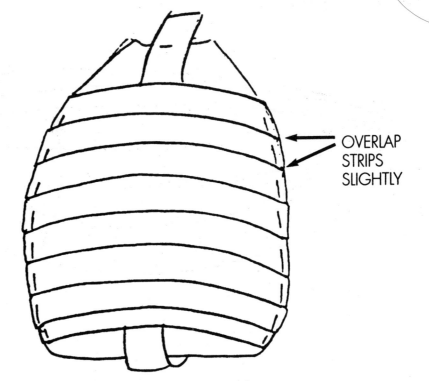

OVERLAP STRIPS SLIGHTLY

BOTTOM VIEW

5.

Slide end under. No need to glue or staple.

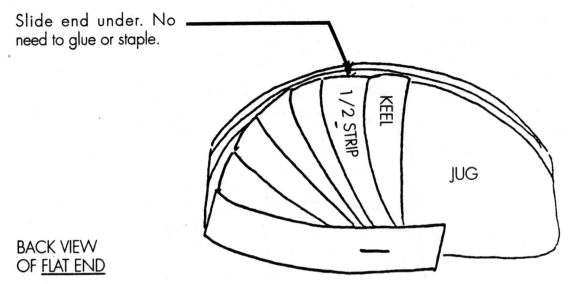

BACK VIEW OF <u>FLAT END</u>

1/2 STRIP

KEEL

JUG

6.

Cut 6 strips in half. Fan out strips to cover flat end.

Fan out 6 strips. Staple at each end.

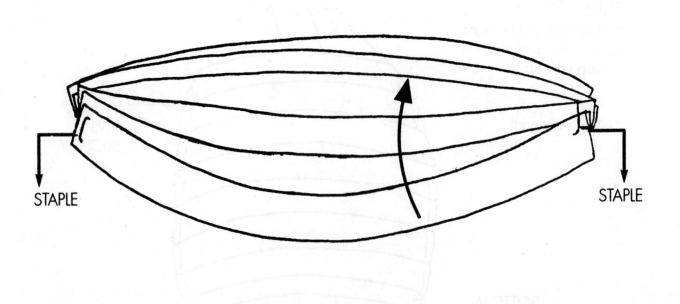

STAPLE

STAPLE

7.

Staple fan to front of ship.

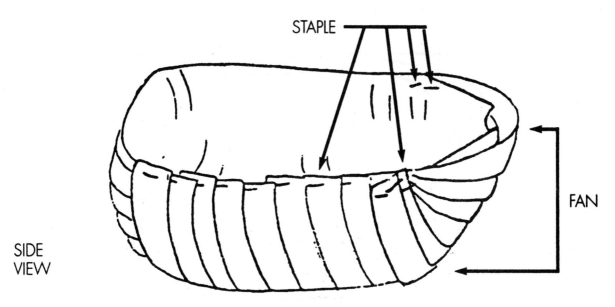

STAPLE

FAN

SIDE
VIEW

8.

Turn ship over. Trace the shape onto an 8 1/2" x 11" piece of tagboard.

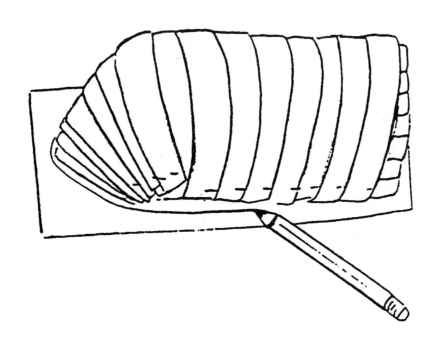

9.

Draw tabs on outline and cut out outline. Do not cut tabs off!

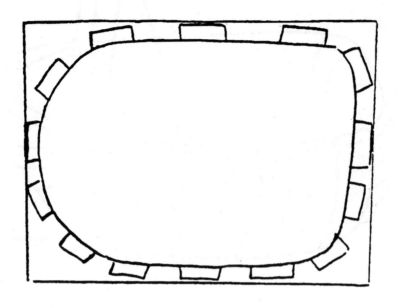

10.

With a pencil, pole 2 or 3 holes (small) for the masts.

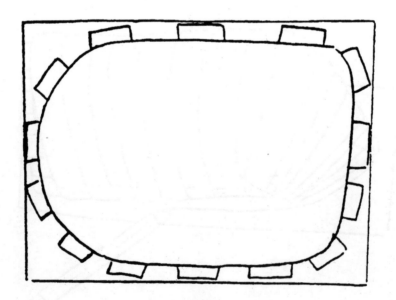

11.

(Looking down into ship)

Have teacher cut 3 "X's" in the plastic jug. These cuts should be the same distance apart as the 3 holes you made in step 10.

CUT HERE

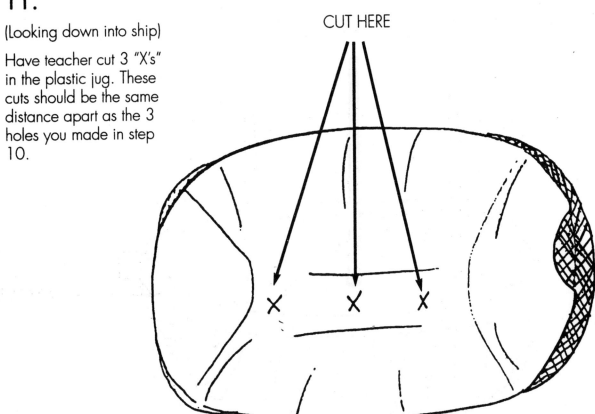

12.

Staple deck to ship. Insert masts. Pinch front so that bow becomes pointed.

INSERT 2 OR 3 MASTS

STAPLE DECK

PINCH

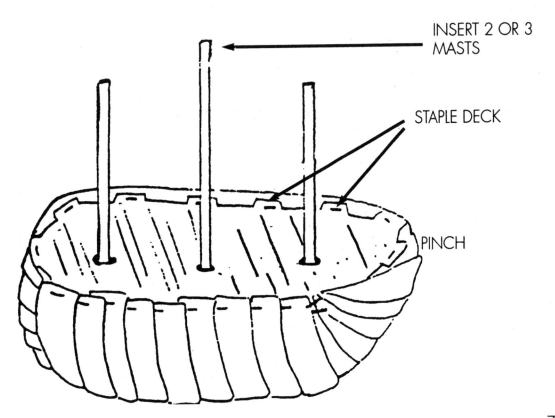

13.

Staple 3 strips around hull.

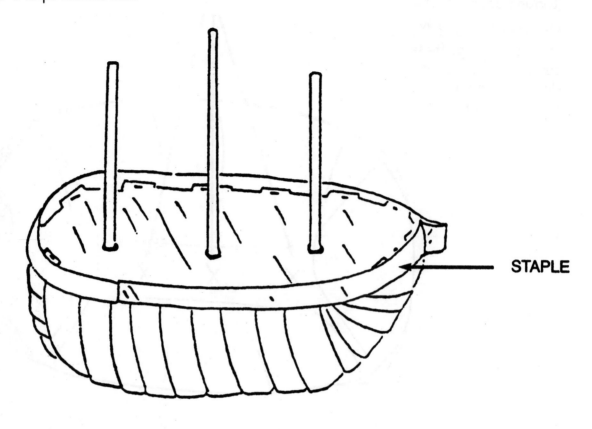

STAPLE

ON TO THE SAILS!

SQUARE SAIL

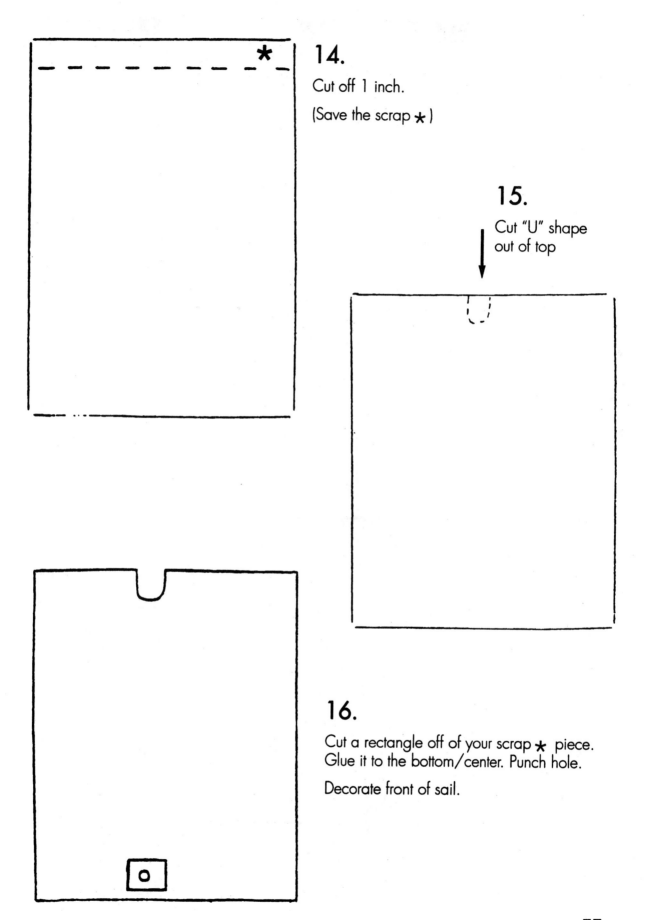

14.

Cut off 1 inch.

(Save the scrap *)

15.

Cut "U" shape
out of top

16.

Cut a rectangle off of your scrap * piece.
Glue it to the bottom/center. Punch hole.

Decorate front of sail.

17.

Fold.

Insert stick.

Glue flap down.

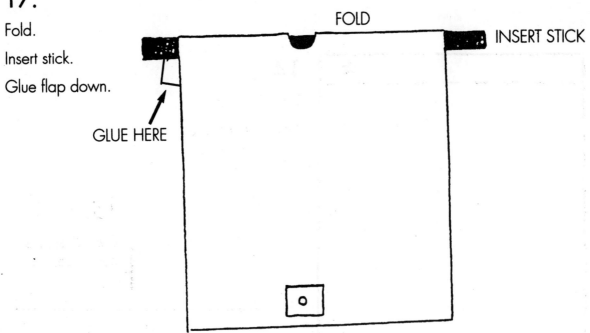

FOLD

INSERT STICK

GLUE HERE

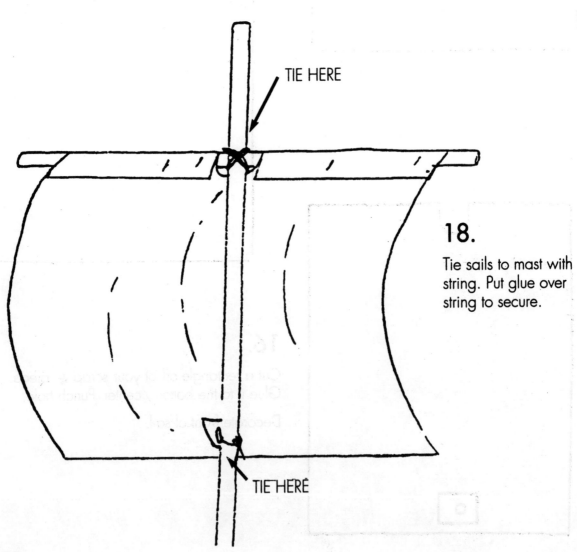

TIE HERE

18.

Tie sails to mast with string. Put glue over string to secure.

TIE HERE

TRIANGULAR SAIL

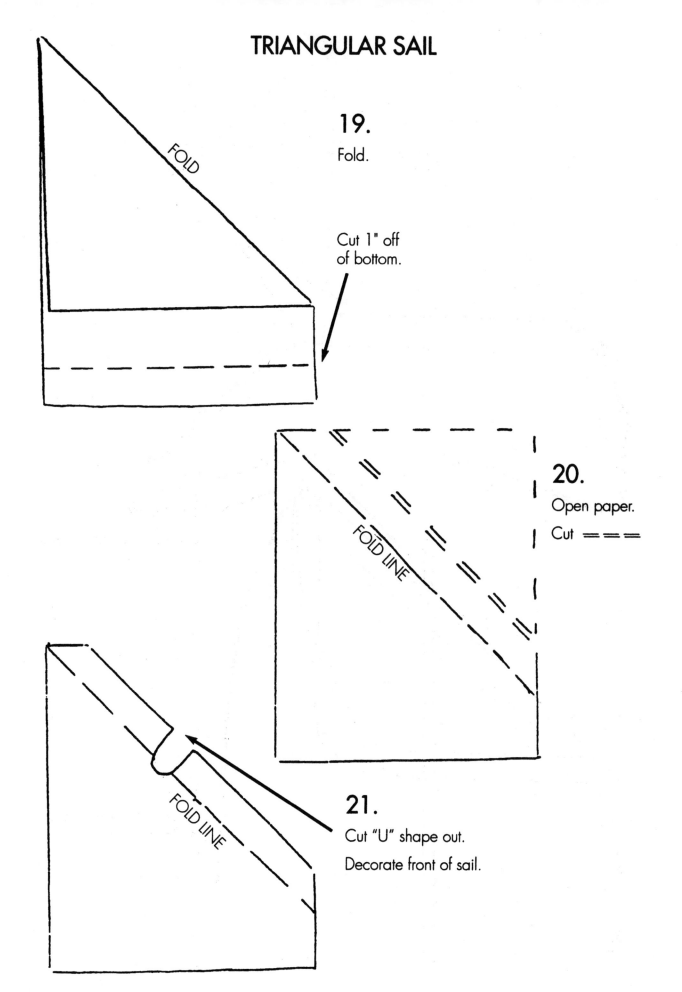

FOLD

19.

Fold.

Cut 1" off
of bottom.

FOLD LINE

20.

Open paper.

Cut ═══

FOLD LINE

21.

Cut "U" shape out.

Decorate front of sail.

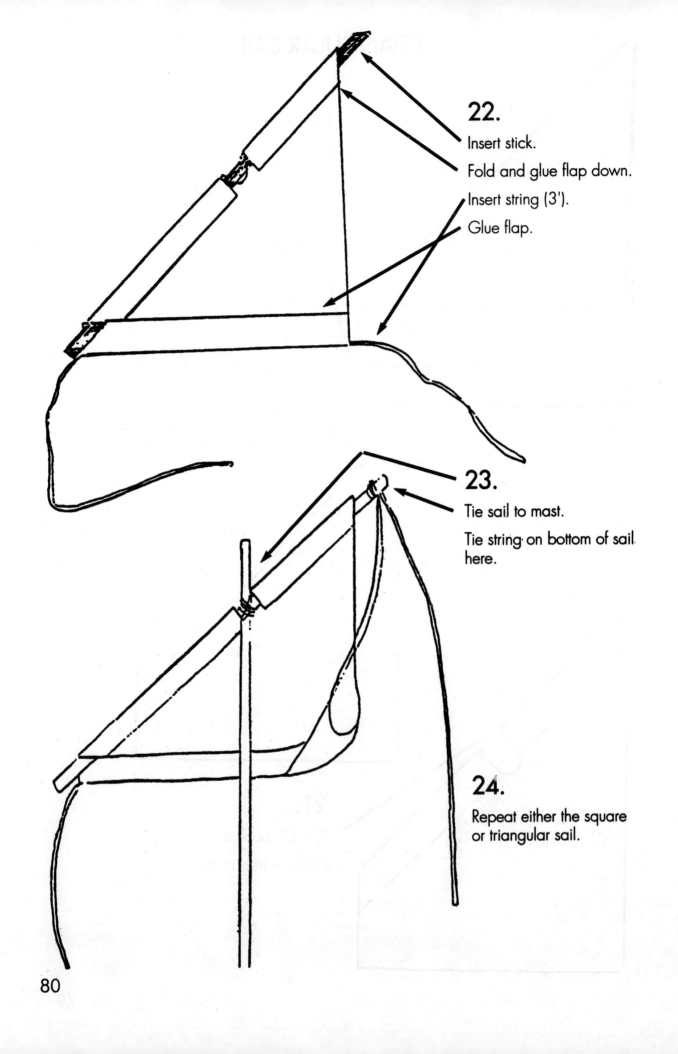

22.

Insert stick.

Fold and glue flap down.

Insert string (3').

Glue flap.

23.

Tie sail to mast.

Tie string on bottom of sail here.

24.

Repeat either the square or triangular sail.

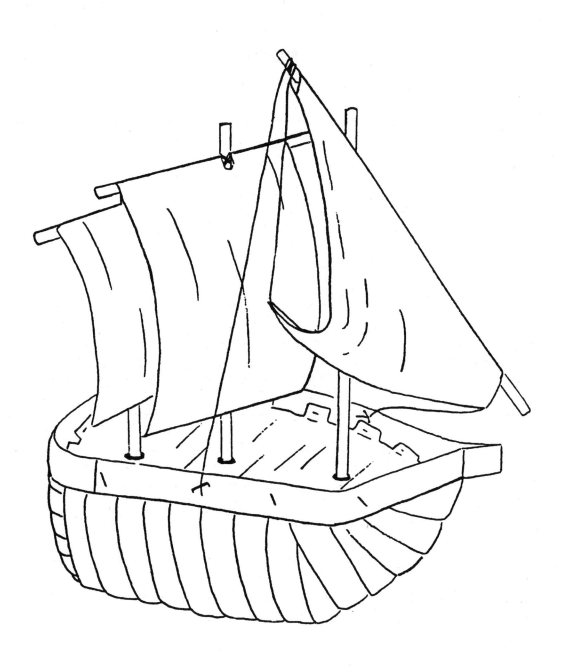

25.
Staple strings of triangular sail to hull of ship.

HAPPY SAILING!

NOTES

NOTES

NOTES